THE WORKING WOMAN BOOK

OR—HOW TO BE EVERYTHING TO EVERYONE

THE WORKING WOMAN BOOK

OR—HOW TO BE EVERYTHING TO EVERYONE

BY: BARBARA & JIM DALE

Andrews, McMeel & Parker

A Universal Press Syndicate Company

Kansas City · New York

Recycled Paper Products, Inc., Edition

This is dedicated to the one I love.

The Shirelles
1961

Ditto.

Barbara and Jim Dale
1985

There was one thing that always kept us going. The advance check.
Also, some real nice people helped.

John Burkoff	Bonnie Kantor
Andy Dale	Mike Keiser
George Diggs	Donna Martin
Phil Friedmann	Steve Perrin
Joanne Fuller	Elaine Ravich
Ann Gallant	Elizabeth Ruffin
Cathy Guisewite	Rhoda Weyr

First Printing, February 1985
Second Printing, May 1985

2 3 4 5 6 7 8 9

THE TABLE OF CONTENTS

(One of the few tables in your
house that doesn't need dusting.)

All women are working women.

PROLOGUE:
THE EVOLUTION OF
THE WORKING WOMAN

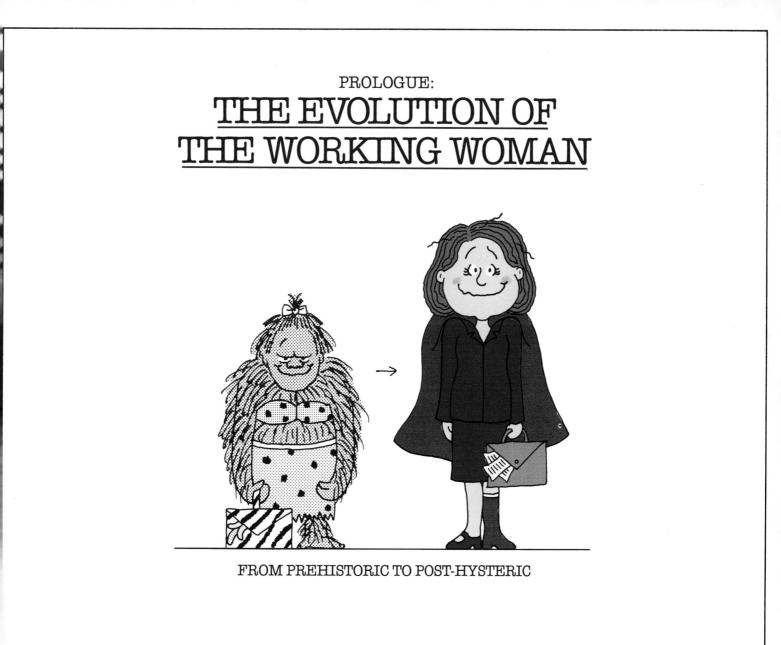

FROM PREHISTORIC TO POST-HYSTERIC

In the beginning, women had two choices: Cavewife, who spent hours over a hot fire, scrubbed loincloths on rocks, polished the family wheel, and did all the grocery hunting. —Or— Working Neanderthal, who rose at the crack of civilization, dropped the kids at Cro-Magnon daycare, and then had to deal with a boss who acted like an ape, because he probably was one.

During the Dark Ages damsels were constantly being snatched into the lascivious clutches of hideous dragons who breathed fire on these poor maidens' chastity belts. Meanwhile, knights were safe inside metal suits, carrying enormous lances, riding speedy getaway horses. And at the end of the day, who do you think had to set the Round Table?

It was somewhat unpopular to be a working woman in Colonial days. In fact, they were called witches. However, in the more enlightened but prudish Victorian times they were known as sluts. (Historians will note that these were not the best of times for working women.)

| 700 BC | 1400 AD | 1850 AD |

CRO-MAGNON CAVE-KEEPER

MEDIEVAL WORKING DAMSEL

VICTORIAN RUFFLED-SKIRT IRONER

In the fifties television perpetrated the myth that all women stayed home and dusted while Ward Cleaver went to the office and Ozzie Nelson took the boys to the malt shop. The truth was, Lucy was the power behind Desi and even father knew that Mother Knew Best.

Today, Working Woman has arrived, the overnight success that took two thousand years.

1950 AD

1970 AD

1985 AD

'50'S WAXY YELLOW BUILD-UP REMOVER

MODERN, BUT TIRED WORKING WOMAN!

1.
BALANCING YOUR HOME LIFE AND YOUR CAREER

OR
THE CHALLENGE OF JUGGLING A CHAIN SAW, SIX POTATOES, AND TWO BUICKS WHILE STANDING ON ONE LEG OF AN UPSIDE-DOWN CHAIR.

Balance, according to physics, is the relationship between two objects kept in perfect equilibrium by a natural or human force. It is also noted that true balance has never been achieved. It's only a theory.

I AM WORKING WOMAN.
I TAKE CARE OF A HOME.
I HOLD DOWN A JOB.

Balancing is a simple concept. Think of it this way. Your family is on one side. Your career is on the other side. You are in the middle. Each side has a rope tied around your waist. They're going to pull in opposite directions.
Get it now?

IN ORDER TO JUGGLE YOUR WORK AND HOME RESPONSIBILITIES, CERTAIN SACRIFICES MUST BE MADE ...

... SUCH AS SLEEP.

Speaking of balancing, Eve said
to Adam, "<u>You</u> try working all
day in the Garden, coming home,
and making a gourmet dinner
every night."

BALANCING A JOB AND A FAMILY IS NOT THE HARDEST THING TO ACHIEVE. IT'S SECOND.

(RIGHT AFTER WORLD PEACE.)

The Five Rules of Career and Home Life Balancing
(or Ms. Murphy's Laws)

1. Doing any two things at once screws up both.
2. At any given time, there is a crisis about to happen.
3. Your family always comes first ...
4. ... Except when your job does.
5. Working Woman was too tired to write a fifth rule.

What's the difference between a Working Woman and a beat-up, rusted-out '54 Chevy?

The Working Woman still has to make dinner when she gets home and the Chevy gets to rest in the garage.

QUESTION:

IS IT POSSIBLE TO PERFECTLY BALANCE A SUCCESSFUL CAREER AND A HAPPY HOME LIFE?

ANSWER:

The famous Flying Wallendas were renowned for their feat of balancing seven Wallendas on a thin shaft of wood supported only by four Wallendas who were in turn carefully balanced by two hearty Wallendas beneath whom was but one lone, strong, reliable, determined Wallenda ...

undoubtedly Mrs. Wallenda.

2.
HOUSEWORK

YOU KNOW WHEN YOU GET UP IN THE MORNING AND YOU
SEE THE MOST BEAUTIFUL SUNRISE YOU'VE EVER SEEN
AND YOU SAY TO YOURSELF FOR EVERY WONDERFUL THING
GOD MAKES THERE MUST BE A BAD THING ...
WELL, THAT'S HOUSEWORK.

Housework is defined as work done
in a house ... which makes the home
a workhouse ... which is often
synonymous with the big house or
prison ... which proves that housework
certainly ought to be against the law.

HOUSECLEANING CAN BE ACCOMPLISHED ALONG WITH A JOB BY CAREFULLY SCHEDULING IT.

SAY, ONE DAY A YEAR.

The Basic Theories of Housecleaning:

The Small House School holds that if a home is tiny enough you can clean it faster than it can refilth itself.

The Large Housers maintain there is a finite amount of dirt per family which should be spread into the maximum number of rooms.

The Ranch House Believers say dirt that is disseminated across horizontal planes may be mistaken for brown shag carpet.

The Three Storyites insist that gravity causes dirt to fall to the basement, where no one sees it anyway.

And, of course, the Mobile Homers simply move from state to state leaving a little dirt in each one.

When doing your housecleaning, be thankful for today's modern products. Just think, we have dishwashing detergents (liquid soap), cleansers (dry soap), laundry detergents (powdered soap), scouring pads (built-in soap), floor polish (pourable soap), and even oven cleaners (strong soap).

In the old days they only had soap.

BEHIND EVERY WORKING WOMAN...

... IS AN ENORMOUS PILE OF UNWASHED LAUNDRY.

Great Rationalizations for Not Doing Housework

1. What's under the rug will only
   be seen by the cockroaches.
2. Penicillin would never have
   been discovered if refrigerators
   were cleaned out regularly.
3. If you vacuum too well,
   what will the cat eat?

I'M NOT DOWN IN THE DUMPS ...

<u>Six Important Things to Keep in Mind About Housework</u>

1. Housework is stupid.
2. Housework is crummy.
3. Housework is lousy.
4. Housework is dumb.
5. Housework is a waste of time.
6. Shouldn't something this wonderful be shared?

THANKS TO WORKING WOMEN, THOUSANDS OF MEN...

... HAVE LEARNED TO VACUUM.

If you ever return from work,
open the front door, and find
yourself in a spotless, sparkling,
perfect home ...

... you're at someone else's house.

3.
THE WORKING WOMAN'S GUIDE
TO MEAL PREPARATION

OR
THREE MINUTES AND IT'S LUNCH.
FIVE MINUTES AND IT'S DINNER.

When doing your grocery shopping, remember, cooking is a vastly overrated concept. Many foods are better uncooked. For instance, carrots, celery, lettuce, all citrus fruits, and berries. Cooking actually removes nutrients from foods and wastes your valuable time. So, as you fill up your shopping cart plan quick healthful meals such as raw liver, cold potatoes, and a bowl of cookie dough.

THE WORKING WOMAN'S GROCERY SHOPPING LIST

Instant Coffee

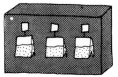

Instant Tea

Instant Orange Juice

Instant Soup

2-Minute Turkey Dinner

1-Minute Stew

30-Second Spaghetti

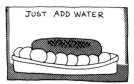

4-Second Meatloaf

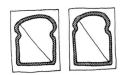

Thaw n' Serve Sandwiches

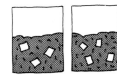

Heat n' Eat Meats & Treats

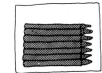

Boil n' Chew Asparagus

Stir n' Swallow Potatoes

Superfast Lasagna

Extra Quick Pork & Beans

Really Speedy Liver

Jiffy Pop Popcorn

Cookbooks offer many delicious meal ideas. Unfortunately they all require something called a recipe. A recipe requires ingredients, utensils, and preparation.

You will never have the ingredients you need (quick, find your turmeric), you won't have the right utensils (where's your copper whisk?), and you can't possibly have time to make the meal (preheat oven at 325° for six days). To make matters worse, all recipes will do one of the following: a) fall, b) overflow, c) burst, d) ooze, or e) turn to ash.

Look for cookbooks in the fiction section of your library.

IF YOU WONDER WHAT TO SERVE FOR DINNER AFTER A LONG DAY AT WORK JUST REMEMBER THE THREE "SOMETHINGS":

1. OPEN A CAN OF SOMETHING

2. THAW OUT SOMETHING

3. PICK UP SOMETHING

One of the most popular phrases in American history is "like my mother used to make." This phrase is always uttered by men to women. It is a gentle but pointed prod to cook something complicated, time-consuming, and usually not all that tasty. A good defense is to suggest the man make "it" himself. Don't worry, he won't. Because nowhere in history do we find the expression "like my father used to make."

A "meal" is an abstract idea. It has no strict definition, no rules, no regulations. A meal is simply whatever one eats at mealtime.

A meal may be a delicate veal cutlet sautéed in lemon and white wine, accompanied by mixed green salad with herb dressing, braised asparagus, fresh-baked crusty Italian bread, followed by chocolate soufflé de menthe and a cup of espresso. A meal may also be the odd half of a hotdog bun, a large spoonful of Skippy Peanut Butter, and a slug of Hawaiian Punch.

So the next time your family says, "What is it?" hold your head up with pride and say, "A meal!"

Every family appreciates a
home-cooked meal. Perhaps
your family will be invited
to someone's house for one.

4.
<u>RELATIVES,</u>
<u>THE GUILT MAKERS</u>

It is essential that your relatives understand how important having a career is to you. Sit down with them, explain it, reveal your feelings, answer their questions, let them really see how much it means to you. If that doesn't work, buy each of them an expensive gift with the money you earn.

IN TIME YOUR RELATIVES WILL COME TO ACCEPT THE IDEA THAT A CAREER IS AS IMPORTANT TO YOU AS YOUR FAMILY.

OF COURSE, IN TIME THE POLAR ICE CAP WILL MELT.

Never complain to relatives about the extra burden of being a working woman. If you do, they will dredge up a relative you've never heard of. Aunt Loretta.

Loretta was National Security Adviser during the Cold War, always served a hot meal, raised twelve perfect children, and did brain surgery as a hobby ... so if Aunt Loretta could do it, what are you complaining about?

DO NOT BRING YOUR OFFICE PROBLEMS HOME.

AFTER ALL, MEN NEVER DO THAT, DO THEY?

You may think you have a first name. Once you go to work that name will be changed by your own mother. Your new name will be "my-daughter-with-a-job" ... as in "This is my-daughter-with-a-job who used to come to see me more often" ... and as in "So, my-daughter-with-a-job, did you break your telephone dialing finger at that fancy job of yours?" ... and especially as in "Oh, your daughter has three lovely children, how nice. My-daughter-with-a-job has a job."

THIS IS MY DAUGHTER WHO STARTED AT THE BOTTOM
OF HER COMPANY AND ROSE TO BECOME A SUPERVISOR
IN ONLY TWO YEARS, SET THE NATIONAL SALES RECORD
THIS YEAR, HAS BEEN ASKED TO JOIN THE BOARD OF
DIRECTORS, AND WHOSE HOUSE IS A MESS.
I DON'T KNOW WHERE I WENT WRONG.

There is hardly anything more critical than having a good understanding with your husband or boyfriend about the importance of your job, about sharing responsibilities, about give and take.

Of course, even if he tries his best to be open-minded, he is facing two thousand years of opposite tradition and he will be called a ''wimp'' at his office.

THE ANNUAL "HUSBANDS-OF-WORKING-WOMEN" CONVENTION

(ALL THREE OPEN-MINDED HUSBANDS IN THE WESTERN HEMISPHERE MEET AND DISCUSS THEIR FAVORITE HOUSEHOLD CLEANSERS.)

In-laws are called in-laws because they
will never let you forget that they are
"in" the family and you are "out" of
the family ... which, of course, makes
you an outlaw.

IN EVERY FAMILY FILLED WITH RELATIVES WHO DISAPPROVE OF YOU WORKING, THERE IS ALWAYS A SECRET BOOSTER.

Do you know why relatives inflict guilt on working women?

Because it works.

5.
RAISING CHILDREN

THE THANKLESS TASK THAT ALSO LEAVES STRETCH MARKS.

If it was going to be easy to raise kids, it never would've started with something called "labor."

WHICH IS THE CHILD OF A WORKING MOTHER?

CHILD
A.

CHILD
B.

From the Terrible Twos to the Terrifying Teens, it's not easy to raise children. There's no escaping it. But you <u>can</u> go to work and put it off until six o'clock each night.

THERE WAS AN OLD WOMAN WHO LIVED IN A SHOE. SHE HAD SO MANY CHILDREN SHE DIDN'T KNOW WHAT TO DO.

SO SHE TOOK A JOB AND HIRED A MAID.

There is a great controversy today over whether leaving a child with a babysitter all day builds independence and strength or causes huge insecurities and neuroses. Oh well, someday you'll know.

FINDING SOMEONE INTELLIGENT, KIND, AND RESPONSIBLE TO CARE FOR YOUR CHILDREN IS QUITE FEASIBLE.

IT WILL COST YOU APPROXIMATELY TWICE WHAT YOU MAKE.

The first step in a good relationship with your children is memorizing their names.

DO NOT BE ALARMED IF YOUR CHILDREN DON'T RECOGNIZE YOU OR REFER TO YOU AS "THAT LADY."

THE SAME THING HAPPENS TO WOMEN WHO SERVE EXTENDED PRISON SENTENCES.

There is no such thing as a wrong way to raise children. Some turn out good. Some turn out bad. And you never know which are which until they're at least twenty-seven.

CONSISTENCY IS IMPORTANT IN CHILD REARING. IF YOU GO INTO A FLYING RAGE WITH ONE OF YOUR CHILDREN, BE SURE YOU GO INTO A FLYING RAGE WITH ALL OF YOUR CHILDREN.

Children not only learn from their parents but parents often learn from their children. This explains why some working women have been known to spit at the boss and call him a ''booger.''

RAISING CHILDREN SIMPLY MAKES HOLDING DOWN A JOB MORE CHALLENGING.

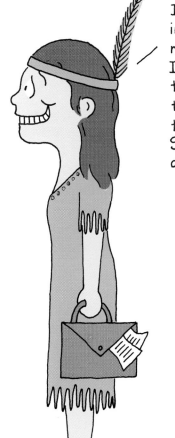

I know we have an important client meeting today but I'm the leader of the Waterfall Princesses this year and I have to go to the Squaw-Scout Pow-Wow at noon.

There is no scientific proof that a woman who has a career will have her children turn out bad.

There's also no proof that a woman who stays home and gives her life to her children will have them turn out good.

In fact, when it comes to children, there's no proof of anything. Good luck.

6.
<u>LOOKING THE PART</u>

<u>OR</u>
DRESS FOR DISTRESS.

Appearance is 90 percent of success. Let's say two women want to sell you something. One looks neat, well-dressed, and well-coiffed. The other looks disheveled, distraught, and generally dismantled. Which would you buy from? Right, the one you can identify with. Clearly, she's more desperate to make a sale.

ANATOMY OF A WORKING WOMAN

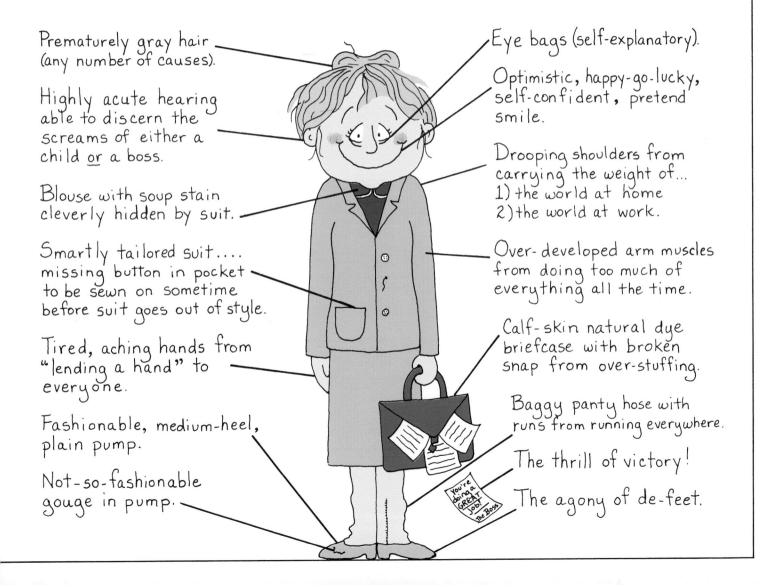

Prematurely gray hair (any number of causes).

Highly acute hearing able to discern the screams of either a child <u>or</u> a boss.

Blouse with soup stain cleverly hidden by suit.

Smartly tailored suit.... missing button in pocket to be sewn on sometime before suit goes out of style.

Tired, aching hands from "lending a hand" to everyone.

Fashionable, medium-heel, plain pump.

Not-so-fashionable gouge in pump.

Eye bags (self-explanatory).

Optimistic, happy-go-lucky, self-confident, pretend smile.

Drooping shoulders from carrying the weight of...
1) the world at home
2) the world at work.

Over-developed arm muscles from doing too much of everything all the time.

Calf-skin natural dye briefcase with broken snap from over-stuffing.

Baggy panty hose with runs from running everywhere.

The thrill of victory!

The agony of de-feet.

You're doing a GREAT job! The Boss

Dressing on a Budget.

The key is to select versatile clothing.
Example, the multiple outfit outfit:
Skirt matches jacket which coordinates
with slacks which go with blouse that
also goes with skirt. Jacket has
removable sleeves to become vest.
Sleeves may be worn as gloves. Vest is
reversible, one side business, one side
down-filled. Skirt can be thrown over
shoulders as cape or draped over head
as veil in case of last-minute funeral.
Slacks can be shortened to shorts using
thigh zippers. Former pants legs may
be wrapped around head as turban or
twisted several times to become belt.
Jacket turned inside out becomes short
formal evening gown. Entire outfit is
inflatable and can be used as life raft in
event of flash flood.

<u>A NOTE OF CAUTION ABOUT GROOMING:</u>

NOTHING THAT IS ORDERED FROM A MAIL-ORDER CATALOG EVER FITS.

Put your best face forward. Every morning, put on a happy face ... even if it takes a putty knife and six pounds of face goo. On the face of it, it may seem superficial, but try a super facial. And never, never let anything look as plain as the nose on your face. Because face it, you're going to come face to face with faces who will look you right in the face. So face the music and use every trick there is. You can save face! (See hints on facing page.)

BEAUTY AIDS FOR THE WORKING WOMAN

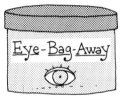

Eye-Bag-Away

Lets you look like people who sleep at night.

LOOKS "JUST-WASHED" HAIR SPRAY

For those few days when you don't have time to wash your hair. (Don't use more than 7 times per week.)

INDOOR TAN

Eliminates the pale green color of people who never see the sun.

Sweat-Never anti-perspirant

Simply closes all body pores once and for all.

156 HOUR MASCARA

Won't come off even if you die.

LIP-SHEEN-SHINE-SLEEK-SLICK

Gives you that sexy, just came in out of the rain look, that no one you know has ever had.

WRINKLE-WIPER-OUTER

Makes you look your age... instead of 10 years older.

INDESTRUCTO NAILS

A combination of crushed diamonds and NASA missile material that won't chip, crack, or burn off during nuclear attack.

The secret to good grooming is ... hiding. Hiding the things that allow you to look "together" when you're falling apart. And the secret to hiding is the Closet Principle, which states: A closet is the best hiding place. A purse is a portable closet. And a briefcase is a closet disguised for business.

Taking advantage of life's closets you can hide the make-up that lets you look wide-awake when you're asleep on your feet ... the unwashed, unpressed, unpleasant-smelling clothing when you're wearing the last decent thing you own ... the hip cinch that you use to keep your bulging thighs from becoming a pedestrian hazard.

Never, never let anyone else look in your hiding places. It is better to be a presentable myth than an honest mess.

THE WORKING WOMAN'S PURSE

MONEY
- One uncashed paycheck.
- Bounce notice from bank.
- $300 in change for parking meters.

APPAREL
- Two extra pair of pantyhose (both with runs).
- One glove.
- 632 hair pins.
- A belt that will fit after your diet.

WALLET
- Expired driver's license.
- Out-of-date gasoline credit card.
- Registration from a car you no longer own.
- Your baby niece's picture.

COSMETICS
- Broken lipstick.
- Cracked mirror.
- Toothless comb.
- One contact lens.
- Nail polish (open in bottom of purse).

BUSINESS
- Memo for meeting dated 10/14/78.
- Report to be filed after nail polish is removed.
- Want ads.
- Two business cards from people who you don't remember.

DOCUMENTS
- Carry-out menus from Rib Palace, Uncle Choo's China Heaven, The Chicken Garage, Fasta Pasta, and Greek Delight (closed by Health Department).

The frizzies. Dishpan hands. Unsightly panty lines. Split ends. Cellulite. When was the last time a working man had to worry about this crap?

7

<u>EXERCISES FOR</u>
<u>THE WORKING WOMAN</u>

<u>OR</u>
THIN NERVES IN THIRTY DAYS

Exercise is the opposite of extra-size.

THE WORKING WOMAN'S EXERCISE #1:

LEAPING OUT OF BED
15 MINUTES LATE:

DING!

(Sharpens reflexes, builds calluses on heels and soles.)

The fitness craze has taken over in the past few years. This is unfortunate, because it replaced the fatness craze.

THE WORKING WOMAN'S EXERCISE #2:

DUSTING AND IRONING
WHILE GETTING DRESSED:

(Improves eye-hand coordination.
Develops "burning blouse" reflex.)

Remember, you only have to shape up, slim down, and work out if you chow down, bulge up, and sleep in.

THE WORKING WOMAN'S EXERCISE #3:

ACCELERATOR-STOMPING
AND BRAKE-SLAMMING
WHEN HURRYING TO WORK:

SCREECH!

(Tones calf muscles. Limbers neck tendons.)

Nautilus, jogging, aerobics, and
isometrics. Somebody actually thought
up these tortures on purpose.

THE WORKING WOMAN'S EXERCISE #4:

RUNNING ERRANDS ON LUNCH HOUR:

(Eliminates lunch.)

Reminder.

The only difference between fatness and fitness is putting your "I" where your "A" was.

THE WORKING WOMAN'S EXERCISE #5:

PAYING BILLS WHILE
MAKING DINNER:

(Bills cause nausea, resulting in
small, low-calorie dinners.)

Think of the life of the working woman as the decathlon. If you even finish it's a miracle.

THE WORKING WOMAN'S EXERCISE #6:

FALLING INTO BED:

(Flattens tummy. Smoothes face wrinkles.)

People in the Ukraine in Russia are noted for their long lives. And not one of them has ever been seen at 6 A.M. in a sweatsuit and a pair of Nikes.

TO THE WORKING WOMAN ...

... JOGGING IS REDUNDANT.

There is one other important benefit to getting in shape. You can beat up your boss.

8

COFFEE, THE RELIGION

DRINKING IT HOT. DRINKING IT COLD. LIVING ON IT AND NOTHING ELSE. GETTING IT FOR OTHER PEOPLE. GETTING IT FOR MALES IN YOUR OFFICE ... AND THE ART OF SPILLING IT.

Some people c-c-c-can't start their
d-d-d-day without c-c-c-coffee.

Do not ask your secretary to get coffee
for you unless you would get it for him.

COFFEE, YOUR ONLY REAL FRIEND.

Contrary-to-popular-belief-it-doesn't-make-you-hyper-it-just-perks-you-up-a-little-and-also-it-keeps-you-going-a-few-extra-hours-or-days.

9.
<u>TIME PLANNING</u>

SKIP THIS CHAPTER; NO TIME TO READ IT.

THE WORKING WOMAN'S DAILY SCHEDULE

<u>7:00 A.M.</u>: Pry open eyes. Close eyes.

<u>7:02 A.M.</u>: Open eyes. Roll over. Close eyes.

<u>7:05 A.M.</u>: Get up.

<u>7:10-7:18 A.M.</u>: Get dressed, do hair, re-do hair, change clothes, change hair, put on first outfit.

<u>7:20-7:29 A.M.</u>: Clean entire house, do laundry, do dishes, no time for breakfast.

<u>7:30-7:45 A.M.</u>: Fight rush-hour traffic, put make-up on in car, get gas for car, check oil, no time to refill oil.

<u>7:46-8:14 A.M.</u>: Search for place to park, circle the block, lurch into tiny parking space, slither out between cars.

<u>8:15-8:30 A.M.</u>: Run flat-out fifteen full blocks to work.

THE RELAXED, WELL-ORGANIZED, EASY-GOING, TOGETHER WORKING WOMAN.

(THERE IS NO SUCH PERSON.)

<u>8:31-9:42 A.M.</u>: Review yesterday's work, stand in line at copier, go get coffee, correct errors in yesterday's work, get more coffee, make more copies, throw out yesterday's work and start over.

<u>9:45-10:50 A.M.</u>: Start doing extra work for co-worker who is out with flu, curse co-worker who is out with flu, begin feeling woozy from catching co-worker's flu.

<u>10:52-12:00 NOON</u>: Re-do work previously approved by supervisor but now rejected by supervisor's supervisor. Try to meet with supervisor's supervisor for clarification. Discover all supervisors are at supervisors' conference with their supervisor.

TIME-SAVING DEVICES FOR THE WORKING WOMAN

12:05-12:07 P.M.: Go to bathroom. Whew!

12:10-12:32 P.M.: Stop at bank, cover nearly bounced checks, beg for mercy from bank, pick up cleaning without cleaning ticket, mail letters at post office, borrow money for postage from total stranger.

12:35-1:00 P.M.: Rush around to buy gifts and gift wrap. Return black shoes with sequins. Look for blue shoes with straps. Find black with straps, blue with sequins. No time for lunch.

YOU CAN SAVE TIME BY ONLY SHAVING THE LEG THAT WILL BE ON TOP WHEN YOUR LEGS ARE CROSSED.

<u>1:05-2:50 P.M.</u>: Re-do work you thought supervisor's supervisor would accept but rejected instead because supervisor's supervisor's supervisor didn't like it. While working on it, your supervisor encourages you to think more independently.

<u>2:55-4:10 P.M.</u>: Start on added work "you've earned" because of your obvious efficiency. Swear quietly to yourself.

<u>4:12 P.M.</u>: Get coffee. Sip. Yeech! It's from this morning!

<u>4:15-5:00 P.M.</u>: Check work of new worker assigned to you because of your fine job in covering for flu-stricken worker and your ability to satisfy myriad of supervisors. New worker's work is lousy. You take it home to re-do it.

WORKING WOMEN ARE JUST LABORATORY RATS IN A SCIENTIFIC EXPERIMENT DESIGNED TO PROVE THAT SLEEP IS NOT NECESSARY TO LIFE.

<u>5:05-5:35 P.M.</u>: Fight rush-hour traffic. Lose.

<u>5:37-5:47 P.M.</u>: Stop in grocery, wait in Express Checkout Lane. Get caught behind man who cheated and bought 112 items instead of 12.

<u>6:00 P.M.</u>: Arrive home too exhausted to eat.

THE WORKING WOMAN LIVES FOR "SOMEDAY."

6:05-7:15 P.M.: Pay bills, swear a lot. Balance checkbook. Cry a lot.

7:17-9:00 P.M.: Re-clean house, which dirtied itself since morning. Do ironing. Burn favorite blouse.

9:08-10:00 P.M.: Start work you brought home. Brew fresh coffee. Fall asleep next to cup of fresh coffee.

<u>7:00 A.M. NEXT DAY</u> : Start over.

10.
<u>CLIMBING AND DUSTING</u>
<u>THE LADDER OF SUCCESS</u>

Success is a matter of luck. As in, "We gave the job to a man and that's your tough luck."

Success is also relative. So don't be surprised if the boss's relative gets the promotion you deserve.

IF YOU AND A CO-WORKER ARE BEING CONSIDERED FOR A PROMOTION, AND THE CO-WORKER IS MALE, YOU HAVE AS GOOD A CHANCE AS HE DOES ...

... <u>IF</u> HE IS AN EMBEZZLER

Competition between male and female employees is only natural. You want that promotion. So does he. You want that raise. He does too. You want to get ahead. Same with him. And surely the competition will be fair. After all, didn't your boss say, "May the best man win"?

The only difference between a man and woman climbing the ladder of success is that the woman is expected to put it back in the closet when she's finished with it.

FAMOUS QUOTATIONS FROM WORKING WOMAN'S MALE BOSSES

Throughout history women have been striving for success in the working world. Some have become famous. Others have been unsung. One such woman was Eleanor Lert, the first female septic tank cleaner ... which explains why no one wanted to get near her, let alone sing about her.

INSPIRATIONAL WORDS FROM FAMOUS WORKING WOMEN

"When I got up for little Pierre's 2 o'clock feeding I had this idea for radium."

MADAME CURIE

"You think it's easy being First Lady and running an ice cream conglomerate at the same time?"

DOLLY MADISON

"I'm sorry the house is a mess. But I've got to finish this flag before they start the revolution."

BETSY ROSS

"I was one of the first women in banking."

MA BARKER

"Keep singing. We'll be bigger than the Jackson Five."

MARIA VON TRAPP

"I'm ruling Portugal and who do you think is watching Chris's kids while he's away?"

QUEEN ISABELLA

The successful woman today may well find herself in a situation where she is the boss of male workers. Some women are a bit uncomfortable with the role. Some are actually unable to cope with the situation. But most settle in, pat the men on their behinds, and get down to work.

IF YOU FIND YOURSELF IN A POSITION OF AUTHORITY OVER MALE WORKERS, DON'T FLAUNT IT ...

... MUCH

Used to be it was a man's world and a
woman's place was in the home ...
They can kiss that shit goodbye.